WE REMEMBERED

ALL THE LIGHT

WE REMEMBERED

ALL THE LIGHT

Moonda Ortiz

Publisher
Positive Imaging, LLC
http://positive-imaging.com
bill@positive-imaging.com

ISBN   9781951776893

To

Lily, Martha,
Candy, and Suzanne.
Thank you.

Also by Moonda Ortiz

Imago

CONTENTS

DAY ONE   1

DAY TWO   7

DAY THREE   13

DAY FOUR   21

DAY FIVE   27

DAY SIX   31

DAY SEVEN   35

ACKNOWLEDGMENTS   41

DAY ONE

They called it by different names at first: The Day of Brotherly Love in Philadelphia, The Day of Presence in Tucson, The Day of Angels (predictably) in Los Angeles. From Oslo (The Great Unfreezing) to North Korea (The Day of Opening), people were compelled to give a name to the inexplicable event that had miraculously happened to them.

It seemed to sweep over the earth in a kind of wave. There had already been warnings about solar storms, some kind of eruption on the surface of the sun. There were concerns about power grid outages and disruptions of satellite communications. Few people paid any attention to these warnings, which had been commonplace lately and never seemed to amount to much compared to the dire predictions. Thus no one (except perhaps for some psychics and scientists?) foresaw what actually happened when the solar rays hit earth.

It began in the morning as the sun was peeking up over the horizon. For those with a view of it, the sun seemed more intense somehow, more colorful than usual, somehow mesmerizing. Those watching began to feel blissful. As each city and town brightened in the morning sun, a strange, crackling energy came with it. Some people reported hearing a kind of static. Others heard music—otherworldly harmonies and melodies. And even if it was raining, a strong sense of well-being began to percolate within the human population, like a dry sponge soaking up moisture.

People who usually woke up grumpy and harried and groping for coffee or tea arose with a sense of elation, as if they had just won the lottery. They were drawn outside to squint at the sun (many for the first time since childhood), to wave at their neighbors, to smile or dance or sing or whistle. Many people were late for work, but they didn't care. Traffic still got snarled along the freeways, but traffic jams suddenly didn't seem important. People rolled down their windows and chatted with those in neighboring cars. They let others merge in front of them. They didn't try to run red lights.

On the radios and TVs, newscasters started talking about "happy juice." They ignored their teleprompts of dire news and began commenting on how glorious the world really was and how much they valued and respected each other. Listeners were bewildered but found themselves laughing along. Something palpable was sweeping over the land and it seemed to affect everyone. It was suddenly hard to remember what the last fight was about, what the grievances were.

Siblings started sharing and saying nice things to each other. Teachers let their students leave the classrooms. Trading eventually ceased at stock exchanges. Politicians stopped ranting and gave each other hugs. Venomous words disappeared into thin air. Bank loans were easily approved. Farmers opened the gates of confined animals. Thieves abandoned their plans.

It was reported that not a single gun was fired that day. There were no homicides, no drive-by shootings, no police shootings, not even hunting. Where war was being waged, soldiers simply threw down their guns, climbed out of their tanks. Bombers returned to the airfields. Missile strikes were cancelled. Prisoners were released. Songs about war being cancelled broke out among troops. Some spontaneously started walking home. Basic training was suspended.

Nobody claimed that every single person on earth experienced this miracle, at least that first day, but who could not be affected by the sudden outpouring of kindness, generosity, respect, and assistance? Like most everyone else, I was suddenly giddy with excitement and possibility. I didn't understand what was going on. I didn't recognize that it was a worldwide phenomenon. I only knew that some weight was suddenly lifted, and everything seemed lighter and brighter and easy and free. I felt truly happy.

DAY TWO

The next day, everyone awoke to rain. Everywhere. Over the entire earth. The meteorologists, who hadn't predicted it, were astounded and confused. It was all over social media and the morning news. It was raining even in the deserts, they said, a fortunate thing there, because dormant flowers started blossoming in the unexpected moisture and covered the barren land. Many people found joy in it, especially in places of severe drought, and danced about in celebration. It was raining even where there had been snow.

The whole earth suddenly greened up. Birdsong was everywhere. Children and even some adults ran out to splash in puddles. And it smelled . . . heavenly, as if each raindrop were scented with an earthy, flowery fragrance.

The rain was mostly gentle, misty, foggy in places. The usual noise of traffic and sirens and machinery seemed muffled. People talked in hushed tones. The rain did not seem menacing or even dangerous, yet never in the history of the world had it rained everywhere, unless it was true about the great floods that were said to have swallowed the land. What did it all mean, given the bliss of yesterday? I wanted to worry about it, to become fearful, but I couldn't. Somehow it was all too remarkable.

I felt an inexplicable pull to not go to work, so I called in sick at my publishing job. At first, all I wanted to do was stare out the window, watch the rivulets drip down the glass. But the pull led me outside eventually. Many people I didn't know were milling around. Beads of moisture dripped from trees. Frogs and toads came out to play. There were earthworms in the sidewalk cracks. I turned my face to the pearl gray sky and felt the warm rain kissing me. And as I stood there, my clothes getting wet, I found myself weeping— gentle tears at first, then small sobs. Tears began to stream down my face. I didn't know what they were about. I saw that others were crying too, right out in the street. Children were crying, old ladies, young men in jogging clothes, sanitation workers come to pick up the trash, a homeless man on the corner. We looked at each other, bewildered.

The emotion of it all continued to rise. I finally went back to my apartment. Great wracking spasms of grief I didn't even know were in me had risen, and I seemed to have no choice but to experience it all. And still the rain continued.

They later called it The Day of Weeping and Wailing over much of the earth because it wasn't just me or the people in my neighborhood. Eventually it became clear that virtually everyone was affected: medical staff, street workers, factory workers, teenagers, bank tellers, truck drivers, politicians, musicians, newscasters, financial analysts, influencers, scientists, actors, accountants, teachers and students, cooks— millions of people found themselves inexplicably sobbing, no matter who they were, no matter what they had done or didn't do, no matter their work or title or lack of such. It was as if every dark and shadowy thought had risen to humanity's surface to be cleansed and washed away by that penetrating rain. As if all that had been buried was now arising. As if people suddenly felt the enormous destruction humanity had caused the earth and each other. Our very hearts were weeping centuries of pain and loss and grief and mistakes and sorrow.

There was no stopping the flood of it. I didn't remember eating or not. The tears kept coming until eventually I fell asleep on the couch. And even in my dreams, it was raining.

DAY THREE

O n the third day, there was a notice-
able wave of relief as day began
over the earth: rain clouds parted, tears
had dried, and the morning sun washed
the skies with gold. The sun's rays on
the wet earth made rainbows in the
puddles. People went out into the
streets to talk with each other, to make
sense of the previous two days, to cook
food, to spontaneously sing or dance.
Children were running around playing
tag and laughing. It's over, people

thought, whatever "it" was. Back to work, nothing to see here. And wasn't it all so strange?

I was about to go in and dress for work when the rumbling started. The very ground beneath our feet seemed to be trembling. Not in a violent way. There were no buildings falling down or cracks in the streets opening up to swallow cars. Just an almost gentle vibration that I could feel in my bones and a kind of low rumble. We in the streets all stared at each other wide-eyed.

I ran back inside my apartment and turned on the news. Sure enough, as with the other events, reports indicated this was a world-wide phenomenon. Seismographs were vibrating in every country that had them. And yet—unusual in itself—there were no significant tremors, no actual earthquakes or volcanic eruptions.

I called in sick again. Flu, I told
them, lying. At first, I was glued to the
television, watching the coverage of all
that had been going on. But as the
newscasters' voices got more and more
strained, I found myself turning it off.
I felt agitated and restless and had the
sense there was something I needed to
do.

The earth was still trembling.
Even in my third-floor apartment, I
could feel the vibrations rattle the
dishes, rattle my bones. I had been
trying to ignore it, but now I surren-
dered to it and allowed the sensations
to pulse through me. I sat on the couch
and listened to the low, growling hum
of it all, and before too long, I felt
something within me trembling as well,
as if something was beginning to break
loose inside of me. I began to shake,
just like the earth. And though I wasn't
cold, I grabbed a lap blanket from the

back of the couch and threw it over my head.

Because every fear I had ever experienced began to rise to the surface of me: childhood fears of bombs and car accidents and bad grades and bogeymen, the time I thought I had killed my dog, teenage fears of not fitting in, fears of inadequacy, aging, diseases and pandemics and germs, insects, rape, wars, asteroids slamming into the earth, violence, the IRS, of not having enough money or food or love. All of these fears had been shaken loose from the places they were stored inside of me. All of them at once.

I shook as if with a terrible fever. Minutes turned into hours, and still more fears arose: plane crashes, terrorists, death, doctors, buildings collapsing, identity stealers, sleeplessness, poisons, explosions, tornadoes, tsunamis, nuclear annihilation.

I was swept into this Day of Fear as if into a flood. I found out later millions of others were doing the same. People pulled over along freeways, too overcome to drive. Surgeons didn't have the nerve to complete surgeries. Bullies hid in closets. Factory lines shut down. Launches were cancelled. Everything halted and paused while we trembled with everything, real and imagined, that had ever frightened any of us. It was excruciating. It was terrifying.

I felt a pull to sit in the sun and went outside with my blanket and sat on the ground. I wasn't the only one. There were many of us huddled and shaking. But I had a realization that the sun was a being that was alive, and it was somehow helping me, helping all of us. Something was helping us, because as the fears oozed out of me like snaking shadows, they seemed to evaporate. I couldn't stop generating them, but the fears were releasing, winking out of existence, or seeping into the earth. And as more and more of them left me, I began to feel lighter, and more hopeful, and expanded in some way.

I had never realized how many things and people terrified me! I had never felt them all at once. I could see that some were silly or unfounded. No seed I ever swallowed as a child ever sprouted; no car I owned had ever exploded or hurled me over a cliff. Were most, in fact, unfounded? Yet I could not stop the great gush of them. And if I had generated thousands of fears during my lifetime, how many had we generated all together, the humans of the world?

In my dreams that night, I was in a large crowd watching a city parade, the crowd cheering and shouting, the sound of drums and marching bands.

But the parade itself was unlike any other. All the participants were frightening. There were six-foot cockroaches, foam mushroom clouds, masked robbers, demon-like beings, devils, zombies, ghosts, hideous extraterrestrials, gargoyles, movie monsters, giant spiders, dark soldiers, mad scientists, and so on. They were all grinning and waving at the crowd and shouting. I strained to hear what some of them said, and I realized they were saying things like, "So long!" "We're outta here!" "It's been fun scarin' ya!"

The parade seemed endless, as if it lasted for weeks. But finally it was over, and the last snake slithered by, the last gun was fired. The last bit of dream confetti fluttered to the ground. And the people along the streets linked arms in the sudden quiet.

DAY FOUR

I woke up with a start and ran to open the window. What sort of day would it be? I felt strange. I knew it wasn't over yet, that more was coming. Yet after yesterday's spewing of fear, I felt curiously unafraid and very calm.

I took a long shower, then made myself some strong coffee and savored the taste and warmth of it. I tried to call in sick once again, but nobody answered. I felt a strong sense of anticipation.

Soon enough the wind started. If it were a normal day, I might not even have noticed, but after the last few days, I felt attuned to nature in ways I hadn't been before. Gently at first, breezes rustled the leaves outside. Wind came through the window and played in my still-damp hair, bringing a pleasant scent I couldn't place. But gradually it built in intensity, flapping around loose papers and bags, whistling through trees. It wasn't hurricanes or tornadoes or even storms—simply wind.

I drank my second cup of coffee and listened to the sound of it all. I wasn't thinking or feeling. Unlike the previous days of intense emotion, The Day of the Wind seemed to scour all thoughts and feelings away, and I felt curiously blank. I didn't turn on the news. I just sat and looked out my window and witnessed it all. The trees seemed like wild dancers, and I watched them curiously. There were few people in the street.

Gradually, the wind moaning, I became conscious of the sound of my own breath and then the sensation of it in my lungs, the pleasurable pulling in and pushing out of air. A tiny moth flitted about the room, and I realized it was breathing too. I suddenly became aware that everything was breathing—all the other people and animals and even plants were all participating in a sacred exchange of air. Even fish had their own way of breathing. The sound of the wind represented the flowing breath of us all. Our entire planet quivered with breath: gnat breaths, elephant breaths, snail and dolphin and bird and butterfly breaths. We all shared a communion of wind that was caressing the earth outside, a give and take that was a basic component of life.

I savored the ritual of breathing the rest of the morning and through the afternoon. As evening came, I started calling various friends (or some called me). That too, was part of the wind, I realized—the air over the vocal cords that made speech possible. I started humming and singing little nonsense songs for the sheer pleasure of it. Like a human mockingbird, I marveled at all the countless sounds I could make.

Late at night, I finally fell asleep. I dreamt of another parade, this one made up of all the people I had ever met or interacted with. Thousands of people: teachers and classmates from elementary through college, bosses and co-workers from various jobs, lovers I had been close to, friends that had come and gone, my eighth-grade crush, relatives I had loved and relatives that I had fought with—all were there. There were animals in the parade too—dogs and cats and birds I had known, a monkey that once sat on my shoulder. Honeybees and lightning bugs and dragonflies and countless other insects flitted in the crowd as well. But mostly there were humans. It didn't seem to matter if they were alive or not.

I barely recognized most of the people. Store clerks? Bank tellers? Librarians? Neighbors? Waitresses? Attorneys? Car mechanics? Insurance adjusters? I sat alone in a large velvet armchair right on the sidewalk (there was no crowd watching), and all the people in the parade, some dressed in costumes or silly hats, waved at me as they walked by. Most wore various shades of gray, but a few were dressed in white or red. Those in white were people I loved or cared about, and those in red (a larger number) were people I had feared or disliked or felt judgmental about or downright hated. But even those people waved at me in a friendly manner, as if all were forgiven, as if there had never been any disharmony between us. The dream people were singing as they marched, threw their arms about each other, danced around, everyone festive. The parade went on and on, never getting to the end. An astounding number of people populate one's given span of life. People I wished I had stayed in contact with, people I would have liked to have known better. People I interacted with for less than a minute. My parents walked by too, my dad waving a TV remote and my mother a wooden spoon. So many people . . .

DAY FIVE

When I awoke, early enough to go back to work, I could not hear the wind any longer, nor was it raining. I went to the window and pulled back the curtain, curious as to what I would see. The last few days had been wonky, and I didn't know what to expect. I was shocked at first, when it appeared to be snowing—giant fat flakes! Could it be snowing all over the world now? But I quickly realized it wasn't regular snow at all, but flakes of light. Tiny bits of light were silently raining down.

I ran outside to get a better look, tilting my face upward. The light petals floated down and sparkled, fragrant and soft. They fell like kisses onto my hair and face and upraised hands. The sky was a milky white. It was unearthly quiet, as if the bits of light muffled everything, as if it was too wonderous of a thing to even speak. They accumulated on the ground in a sparkling cover, making an ankle-deep blanket of light.

I rushed inside to call in sick yet again—and again no one answered. I turned on the news. There were videos from all over the world. People gathered at the Vatican, their arms and faces uplifted to the rain of light. Soldiers crawled out of tanks with looks of awe. People held hands and cried in Central Park. Others spontaneously gathered at sites like Stonehenge. A child looked joyfully into the camera saying, "Heaven has come."

And then suddenly, as if appearing from another dimension, even inside my apartment the splashes of light dropped like flower petals right out of the ceiling. I glanced at the TV, and it was the same. Bewildered and emotional newscasters caught particles of it in their hands. Traffic had stopped in the streets. Flights were halted. Teachers gathered their students close. Even in the prisons and the hospitals and the POW camps and war-torn regions and the Pentagon the blessed light fell. And from somewhere, many people heard music. Lilting, ethereal, melodic.

There was no question about it now: all that had happened wasn't chance or something strange the earth was going through. This was some sort of—intervention. This was something the likes of which humanity had never before experienced. A strange energy built within me.

How long would the star light rain? I called many of my friends. I went back outside. There was no point in worrying about what would happen. All I could do was experience it as it came. Something opened up inside of me and it seemed as though the light rained there too—into my gut, my heart, my head, my cells. My very electrons seemed to be spinning with this wondrous light. I was flooded with a profound peace unlike any I had ever known. From the looks of my rapturous neighbors, so was everyone else.

DAY SIX

On the sixth day, the sun was streaming in the window when I awoke. No rain, no wind, no more petals of light. Just quiet. Everything seemed to be shimmering in an odd way. And then I noticed that I could see tiny threads that were reflecting the light like a spider web. This gossamer web was attached to everything. I could suddenly perceive a vast network that I had never seen before. It was dizzying.

As I turned away from the window, I saw it in my living room as well. I was immersed in a sea of tiny threads spreading all throughout the room. The network seemed to be moving and floating and I could see tiny creatures swimming in it like miniature stars and orbs. It was spectacularly beautiful.

Out of habit more than anything, I went to make coffee, but the bag of beans, the cup, the spoon—all were gently attached to this web. And when I took a sip, finally, the cup swished the filaments to my face. I didn't know what to make of it all.

After my coffee, I went outside. People were turning and lifting their hands in a bewildered way. Dogs were licking the air. "Do you see it?" a young woman holding a toddler asked me, her eyes wide. I nodded. The tree limbs seemed to reach up into the web and play with it. Each blade of grass, every little stone, radiated tiny threads of light. Everything was shiny and shimmering.

I spent the day wandering around, walking through this magical glistening sea. It made me feel like dancing. I was connected to the sidewalk, to the telephone poles, to the cars and birds and even the sky. The trees had an aura of web around them. I went into a restaurant and watched the little lights play around my waffle, the waitress, the menus, the various customers. I was intertwined with the TV in the corner reporting on the worldwide visions of interconnectedness. If I shut my eyes, I could hear a sea of sounds as well, all now somehow one thing, like notes in a song played by countless musicians: a rooster, a refrigerator humming, a bit of conversation, dishes clinking, bacon sizzling on a grill, coins, straws being slurped through. It was a joyous symphony of life and movement and color and noise, all of it emanating from this planet. And as the earth spun and generated her web, she reached out, enfolding us all, touching the other planets, the stars, the galaxies, unto all that is.

DAY SEVEN

I was surprised to awaken in my own bed, as I didn't remember coming home. I looked around curiously. I could still sense the exquisite web, the tiny, sticky threads of light. I waded through the sea of it to the living room window and looked out. The sun caught me then, bathing my face and I could feel something whirring within. I felt like a clock that had just been wound. My very cells seemed to quiver with energy. Something was activating within.

Then, some kind of explosion of intense light happened inside my heart. It wasn't painful, but blissful. As if a light were lit in a dark cave bringing warmth and comfort. It unfurled out of me feet into the air, reminding me of the light of opals. Everything this sparkling light touched felt ignited.

I ran outside, not even closing the door after me. The first person I saw was a man I didn't know, and we stopped and stared at each other. A galaxy of light was swirling out of him too and it felt both motherly and fatherly. Our lights reached toward each other and blended into one embrace. "I know you," he said, awed. Tears started streaming down his face. "I know you."

We suddenly knew what we had to do: we had to touch everyone and everything with this wondrous, radiating, rainbow light—the trees, the shrubs, the passing dog. And as we went, we gathered others, some still in pajamas. It didn't matter who—a yard worker, a homeless woman, a guy in business suit not wearing shoes—we were drawn to each other like magnets and rushed into each other's arms, and as we did, there were even more explosions of light. It became so bright that people's forms started fading away. We became transparent beings, housing countless stars within our organic membranes. Physical identities of class and race and age, once so important, began to disappear. It felt urgent that everyone be included—no matter if once we had disliked them. Differences weren't important now.

Hundreds, and then thousands of us were in the streets, everyone reaching for everyone else. Whatever normal activities we had were now forgotten.

The sun seemed to be fueling us. Those once estranged cried with joy at reconnecting. We streamed into hospitals and the light we radiated healed afflictions. We danced into shelters, jails, courtrooms, factories, classrooms. Some of us sang and made music. No one was afraid. No one was too poor or disabled or weird or sick to be included. We melted into each other, our hearts expanding.

When night came, we were still in the streets gathering each other. We radiated so much light we didn't need artificial lighting. We celebrated and sang and danced and whooped with joy as we waited for the morning sun. We were like living fireworks. We were one being with billions of facets birthed by a miraculous planet. We were the eyes of Earth, seeing all. And She herself was exploding with love and life and celebration. Blossoms sprang up everywhere. Birds landed on our shoulders. Squirrels scrambled between our feet. Animals came out of woods, drawn to us.

We called it The Day of Remembering because we remembered how to love. We called it The Great Beginning, because we knew all would be different now. We called it The Day the Light Came, because our inner fire had been forever ignited. We called it The Day of Union because we could never be separate again.

ACKNOWLEDGMENTS

Special thanks to Tony Ortiz, always steadfast, and to Sharrin Michael, Robert Test, Linda Galvan, Jeanne Duplantier, Catherine Ruivivar, Ida Claire Bruno, and Gracie Lanni for their encouragement and enthusiasm.

Made in the USA
Columbia, SC
08 September 2024

42013565R00031